Little Kiddy Yoga

For D, J & K
Thanks to Vasudeva

By Jahri Jah Jah!

www.jjj.co.nz

Self published by Shane Rosemeyer
Takaka, New Zealand

ISBN 978-0-9582848-9-9

Yoga

Yoga is the ancient art of balance and unity.
Unity of body mind and spirit.
Children are natural yogis, full of unconditional love,
with open, hungry minds.
Children are eager to learn and grow.
They have a natural ability.
Yoga can help young families develop.
Yoga encourages strength, flexibility, co-ordination,
a peaceful mind, pure food and loving happiness.
This book is an introductionto yoga.
As a parent or teacher you can use this book to guide
the children and to help them explore
their world in a fun way.
Om shanti shanti shanti!
(Om, peace, peace, peace)

Om is the primordial ancient sound and symbol.
It acknowledges waking, dreaming,
deep sleep and trancendental
levels of consciousness.

Om is a pure mantra that is all encompasing.

Chant Om for a few minutes
with your children and observe
the state of peace it brings.

Sun Salutations

The sun is the provider and
sustainer of our life.
Sun salutations are a series
of yoga postures that acknowledges
the sun and awakens our
inner radience.
Sun salutations have many variations.
This sequence is a simple
one to start with
and is simplified for young children.

Swinging Arms

Start by swinging your arms
from side to side for a few minutes
to relax the body.
Keep your arms nice and floppy.

Prayer

Start with centering.
Take a few deep breaths together.
Chant Om if you want 3 times.
This posture is a universal symbol
of prayer and devotion from the heart.

Tree Pose

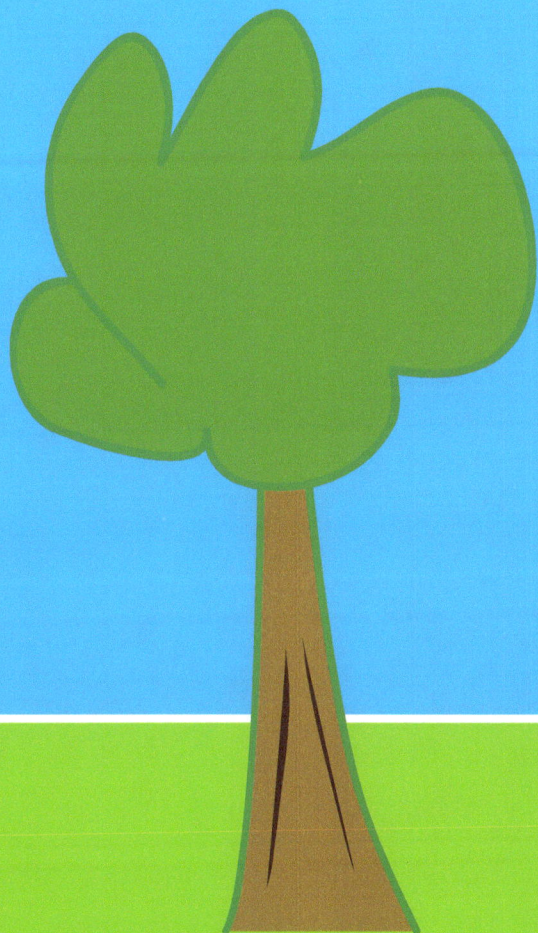

Take a big breath in and reach up tall
and straight like a big strong tree.

Fingers to Feet

Breathe out and bend forward
with your legs straight.
Touch your toes.

Crocodile

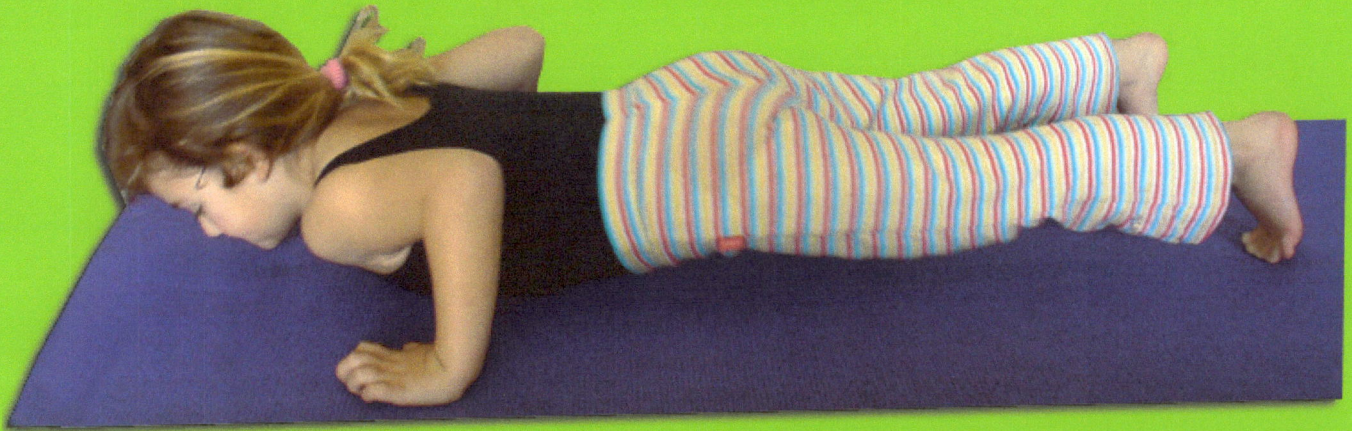

Jump both feet back and lie on your
tummy on the floor.
Push down with your hands and toes to lift
your body up a little.
Just like a crocodile!

Cobra
(upward dog)

Breathe in and rise up into cobra pose.
Arch your back carefully and look up.
Variation: Look back over each shoulder.

Mountain
(downward dog)

Lift your bottom up towards the sky with
straight arms and legs
like a big beautiful mountain!
Variation: Lift 1 leg up high off
the ground, then the other leg.

Now jump your feet forward
to the hands again...

Fingers to Feet

Stand up, back into...

Tree Pose

Prayer ॐ

Deep breath in and start again.
Go through this series 2-10 times.
Make it fun.
Name each posture as you go.
Play calming yoga music if you want.

Butterfly

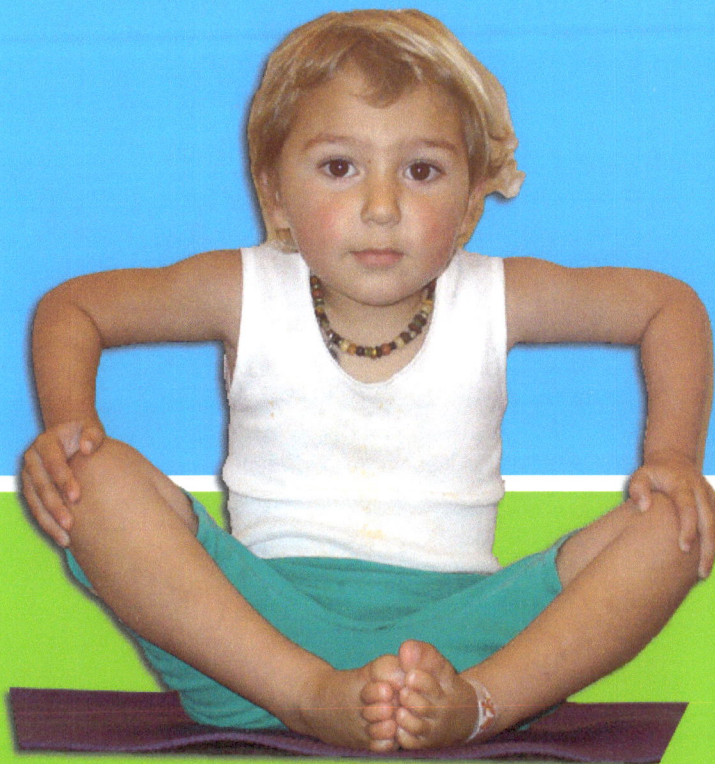

Flap your legs like butterfly wings!

Touch Toes

Legs straight, back straight.
Wiggle your toes.
Variation: Row the boat!

Splits

Legs straight!
Nice and wide.

Spider

Lift up!
Nice and high.

Variation: Lift 1 leg up.
Extend it out straight!

Star

Twinkle like a shinny star!
Stretch your arms out wide.
Feet wide apart. Variation: Twist it!

Triangle

Feet apart and
bend to the side.

Touch
your toes.

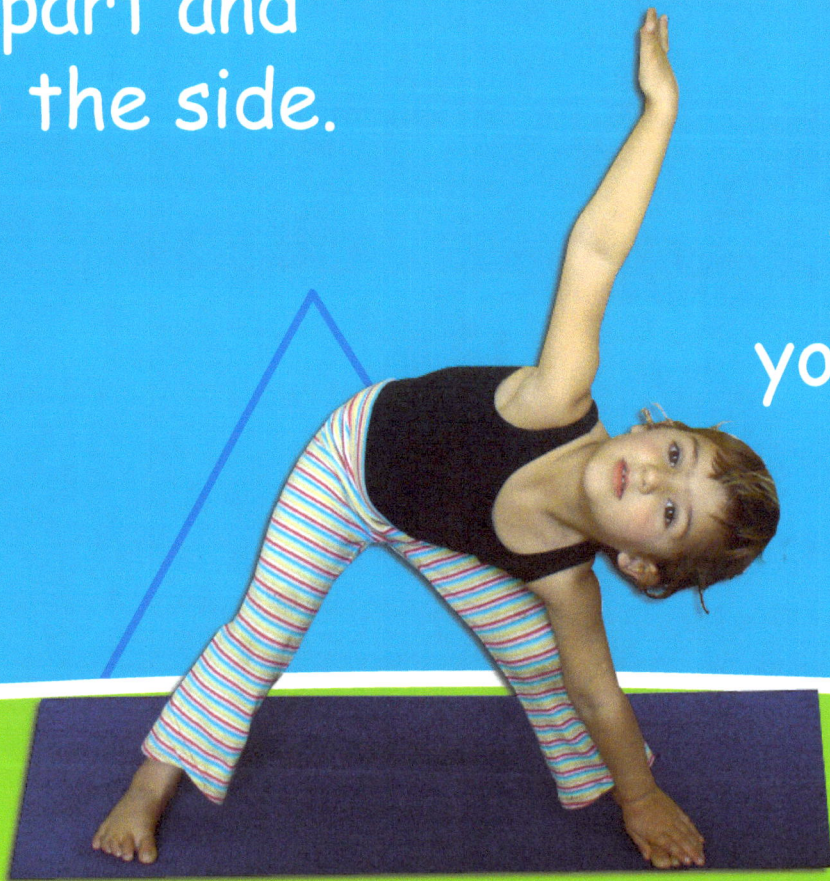

Keep your legs straight.
The other hand reaches
high up to the sky.
Variation: Twist opposite hand to foot.

Aeroplane

Stretch your wings
out wide and fly!
Balance on 1 leg. Swap Legs.

Squat

Squat down.
Try and keep your feet flat.
Put your hands into prayer position.

1/2 Moon

Drop down onto 1 knee.
Step forward with 1 leg
and stretch your arms upto the moon!
Work both sides.

Diamond

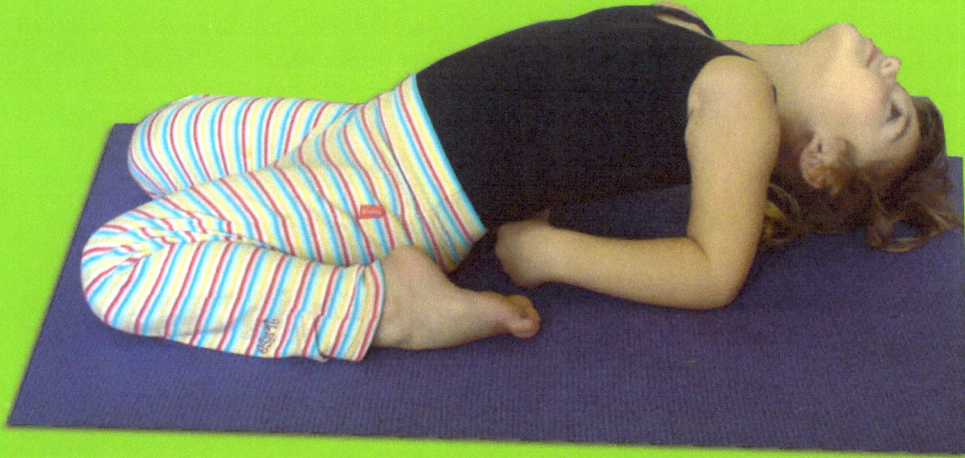

Bend your legs back at the knees
and drop back onto your elbows.
Go back all the way to the floor
if you like and lie flat.

Meditate
(Relaxation)

Lie down on your back like a starfish.
Close your eyes.
Squeeze and relax your fingers,
right side then left.
Screw up your face then relax, 3 times.
Imagine you are heavy like a rock.
Imagine you are light like a feather
and float away.
Meditate quietly for a few minutes.

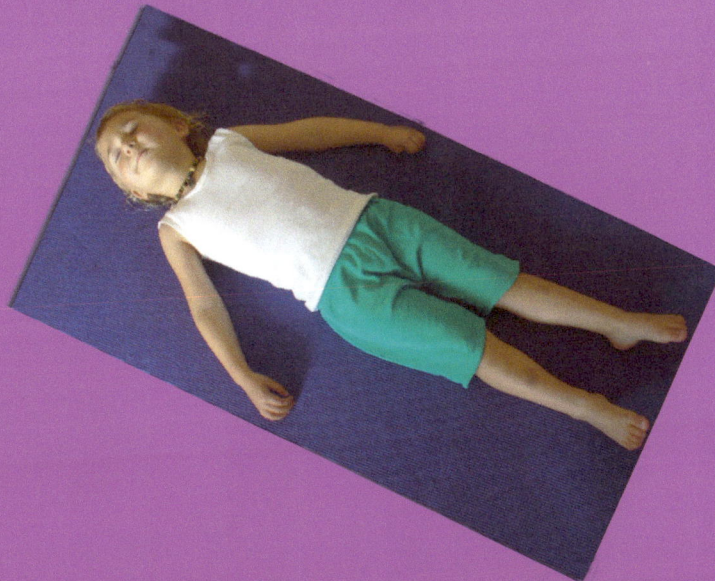

Yogi Food for Children

Eat natural foods!
Fruit vegetables and grains.
Children are growing and need good quality food.
Breakfast: Porridge with banana, raisins, dates, almonds, coconut and molasses.
Whole grain bread, toast with manuka honey, almond butter and jam.
Ghee (clarified butter) is the Yogi spread.
Lunch: Wholemeal sandwich with hummus, cottage cheese, tomato and other fresh salads.
Fresh fruit, home baked cookie or baking made with wholesome ingredients.
Dinner: Basmati rice, quinoa, lentils, tofu, falafel. Sunflower, pumpkin and sesame seeds
Vegetable soup and lentil dals are nourishing and easy to digest. Whole grain pasta,
stir fried vegetables, tofu burgers, burritos and tacos. Flat breads (yeast free).
Natural yoghurt, cottage cheese, and paneer.
Good quality olive oil and cold pressed coconut oil.
Warm whole milk with a pinch of cardamom, ginger or nutmeg to help digestion.
Fruit is best eaten by itself as morning or afternoon tea.
Drink like warm water, herbal teas and diluted juice.
Organic is great. Grow your own veges.
It is just as important to eat in a calm and quiet manner and to chew your food well.
Yogis are vegetarian.
Animals have awareness and feelings. Please respect them.
People are continuing to exploit animals and the environment unnecessarily.
Eat natural whole foods in a medium quantity in a peaceful way.
Drink water and live long!

Jahnu ...almost 3...

Jahri Jah Jah
Dip Ayurvedic Medicine

Daya 4

www.ingramcontent.com/pod-product-compliance
Lightning Source LLC
Chambersburg PA
CBHW041557040426

42447CB00002B/201